EARTH SCIENCE—GEOLOGY Need to Know

SilverTip

Minerals

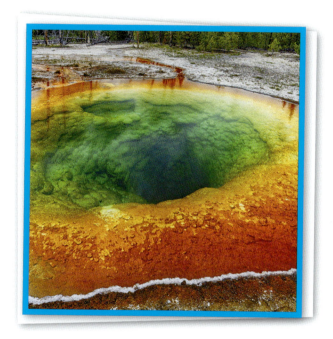

by Ruth Owen

Consultant: E. Calvin Alexander Jr., Professor Emeritus
Earth & Environmental Sciences
University of Minnesota, Minneapolis

BEARPORT
PUBLISHING

Minneapolis, Minnesota

Credits

Cover and Title Page, © Filip Fuxa/Shutterstock; 3, © Damian Pawlos/Shutterstock; 5T, © laamayad omar/Shutterstock; 5M, © fifg/Shutterstock; 5B, © New Africa/Shutterstock; 7T, © Diego Sugoniaev/Shutterstock; 7B, © Albert Russ/Shutterstock; 8, © Holly Mazour/Shutterstock; 9T, © Loekiepix/Shutterstock; 9B, © Albert Russ/Shutterstock; 11, © vvoe/Shutterstock; 13, © Salienko Evgenii/Shutterstock; 14L, © Media Whalestock/Shutterstock; 14R, © Mamuka Gotsiridze/Shutterstock; 15, © Aleksandar Malivuk/Shutterstock; 16, © JAVIER TRUEBA/Science Source; 17, © Mindscape studio/Shutterstock; 18, © Natali Zakharova/Shutterstock; 19, © Joshua Resnick/Shutterstock; 20–21, © Narongsak Nagadhana/Shutterstock; 22, © Denis Radovanovic/Shutterstock; 23, © Misunseo/Shutterstock; 24, © Mark S Johnson/Shutterstock; 25, © Oscar Sweep/Shutterstock; 27, © gabriel12/Shutterstock; 28T, © Nasky/Shutterstock, and © Retouch man/Shutterstock; 28M, © Nasky/Shutterstock, and © vvoe/Shutterstock; 28B, © StudioMolekuul/Shutterstock; and © Chones/Shutterstock.

President: Jen Jenson
Director of Product Development: Spencer Brinker
Senior Editor: Allison Juda
Associate Editor: Charly Haley
Designer: Colin O'Dea

Library of Congress Cataloging-in-Publication Data

Names: Owen, Ruth, 1967- author.
Title: Minerals / by Ruth Owen.
Description: Silvertip books. | Minneapolis, Minnesota : Bearport
  Publishing Company, [2022] | Series: Earth science-geology: need to know
  | Includes bibliographical references and index.
Identifiers: LCCN 2021039171 (print) | LCCN 2021039172 (ebook) | ISBN
  9781636915791 (library binding) | ISBN 9781636915869 (paperback) | ISBN
  9781636915937 (ebook)
Subjects: LCSH: Minerals–Juvenile literature.
Classification: LCC QE365.2 .O94 2022 (print) | LCC QE365.2 (ebook) | DDC
  549–dc23
LC record available at https://lccn.loc.gov/2021039171
LC ebook record available at https://lccn.loc.gov/2021039172

Copyright © 2022 Bearport Publishing Company. All rights reserved. No part of this publication may be reproduced in whole or in part, stored in any retrieval system, or transmitted in any form or by any means, electronic, mechanical, photocopying, recording, or otherwise, without written permission from the publisher.

For more information, write to Bearport Publishing, 5357 Penn Avenue South, Minneapolis, MN 55419. Printed in the United States of America.

Contents

Made of Minerals 4

All About Minerals 6

Cool Crystals 8

The Building Blocks 10

How Do We Get Minerals? 12

Minerals Everywhere 16

Minerals on the Menu 18

Flashy Minerals 22

Caring for Earth's Minerals 26

Inside Minerals 28
SilverTips for Success 29
Glossary 30
Read More 31
Learn More Online 31
Index 32
About the Author 32

Made of Minerals

What do rocks, Olympic gold medals, and toothpaste have in common? They all have **minerals** in them. Minerals are solid **substances** made by nature. Look outside and you probably see them all around. Minerals are also in many things that we use every day.

Fluorite is a mineral found in some rocks. It has fluoride in it. A kind of flouride is added to toothpaste to help keep teeth healthy.

All About Minerals

There are thousands of minerals on Earth. They all share some things in common. All minerals are solid. Also, minerals form **naturally**. Another thing about minerals is that they are not alive and have never been alive.

> Being solid does not mean all minerals are hard. Some are softer than others. Softer minerals may change shape easier. Harder minerals are stronger.

Talc is a soft mineral.

Topaz is a hard mineral.

Cool Crystals

What makes minerals different from one another? Like everything else, all minerals are made of tiny **atoms**. But each mineral's atoms come together in a different shape. These shapes are called **crystals**.

Mineral crystals are often too small to see. But sometimes, crystals come together in larger shapes also called crystals. The mineral quartz forms in large crystals.

The atoms of a mineral called galena (guh-LEE-nah) form in a cube shape.

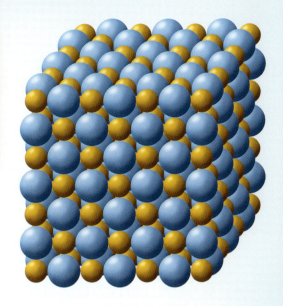

Galena crystals

The Building Blocks

Minerals are in a lot of things around us. They are in many metals. And minerals are the building blocks of rocks. Some rocks are made of just one mineral. Others have several minerals.

Rocks get their colors from the minerals in them. Rocks with more than one mineral are often different colors.

> Granite is a rock that comes in lots of colors. That is because each kind of granite is made from a different mix of minerals.

Different kinds of granite

How Do We Get Minerals?

Rocks that have useful minerals are called **ores**. We can get these minerals through **mining**. First, the ores are removed from the surrounding rock. This may be done by using **explosives** to break up rocky ground. Then, huge trucks carry the ores to factories where the minerals can be removed from unwanted rock.

Sometimes, ores are buried deep in the ground. Workers use machines to dig tunnels down into the rock. Then, they can get the ores.

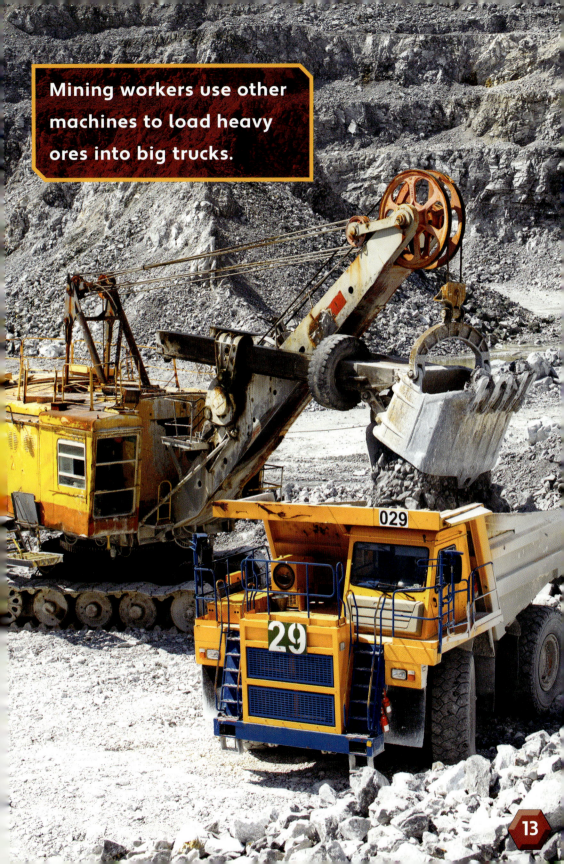

Mining workers use other machines to load heavy ores into big trucks.

Factories have different ways of getting minerals out of ores. Some help us get metal minerals. They often crush the ores into powders to separate the minerals. Sometimes, chemicals and heat are used to remove the minerals from the ores. Then, electricity heats the minerals into liquid metal. As hot liquid metals cool, they harden.

Other factories make metals into objects. Aluminum is flattened and formed into a giant roll. Then, the roll of thin metal is used to make soda cans!

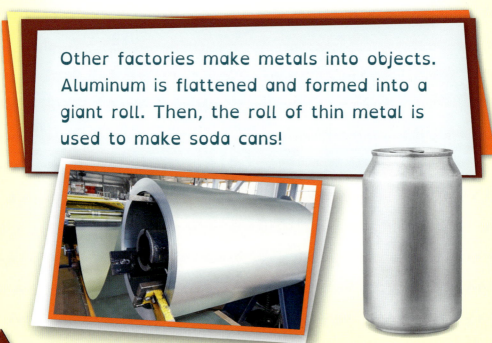

Minerals Everywhere

What can we make out of minerals? They are in so many things, from the streets we drive on to the foods we eat! One mineral we use a lot is gypsum. It is in roads, walls, shampoo, and tennis courts. It is even used to make some foods.

Mining workers found giant gypsum in a cave in Mexico. Some of the pieces were 40 feet (12 m) long!

Minerals on the Menu

We eat some minerals because they are good for our bodies. For example, our bodies need the mineral iron to make blood. But we can't eat minerals as metals or rocks! So, factories add other forms of minerals to many foods. If you had cereal for breakfast today, you probably ate about six forms of minerals!

> Some foods have minerals in them naturally. The minerals do not need to be added. Meat, eggs, and vegetables have iron.

The salt we eat is a mineral that forms in rocks. Some of this salt is dug from the ground through mining. But some of it comes from salty ocean water. To get it, we trap ocean water in smaller ponds. When the water dries up, salt is left behind.

Why is ocean water salty? Some of the salt comes from rain hitting rocks. The rain makes tiny bits of salt break off the rocks and fall into rivers. Then, the rivers carry the salt into oceans.

Workers pile up the salt that is left behind when water dries. Then, they collect the piles so we can use the salt.

Flashy Minerals

Some minerals, such as salt, are common. But others are **rare**. Gold is a rare mineral. This shiny metal is worth a lot of money. People have been mining gold for thousands of years. It is used to make many things, including jewelry and even parts of electronics.

A shiny mineral called pyrite looks a lot like gold. But pyrite is not rare. It was nicknamed Fool's Gold because people found it in rocks and thought it was real gold!

Diamonds are another kind of flashy mineral. They are among the hardest minerals on Earth. These minerals can be used to make strong tools. Diamond tools can cut rock and metal.

The color, shape, and sparkle of some diamonds makes them extra beautiful. The prettiest diamonds are used to make jewelry. Some are worth millions of dollars!

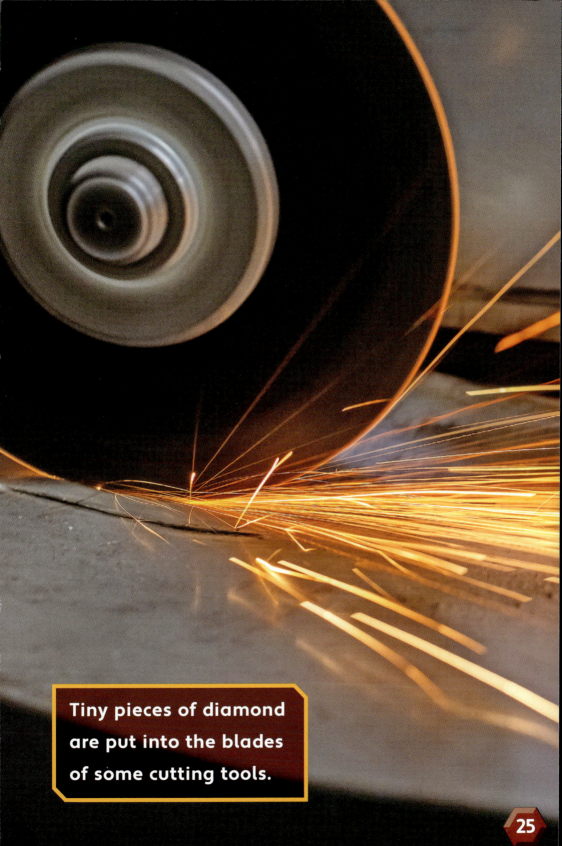

Tiny pieces of diamond are put into the blades of some cutting tools.

Caring for Earth's Minerals

While minerals are useful, we have to be careful. Digging for minerals can hurt the land where plants and animals live. And there is not an endless amount of minerals. Reusing and **recycling** things made from minerals can mean we will have many minerals for the future.

> We use minerals to make millions of new cell phones every year. But do we need to use up our minerals so fast? If more people use their phones for longer, we could save minerals.

Recycling old phones means we can reuse their minerals.

Inside Minerals

Minerals look different depending on how their atoms come together. Let's look at the atoms inside a few minerals . . .

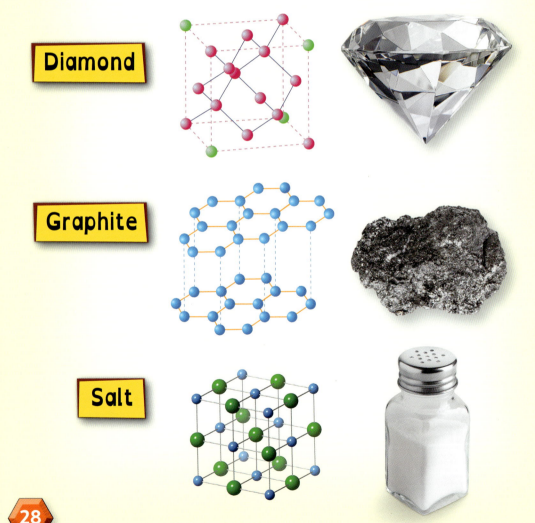

Diamond

Graphite

Salt

SilverTips for SUCCESS

⭐ SilverTips for REVIEW

Review what you've learned. Use the text to help you.

Define key terms

crystalmining
metalores
mineral

Check for understanding

What is a mineral?

What are some things that all minerals have in common? And what is something that is different about different minerals?

How are rocks and minerals related?

Think deeper

What are some ways we use minerals in our daily lives? Why do minerals matter?

⭐ SilverTips on TEST-TAKING

- **Make a study plan.** Ask your teacher what the test is going to cover. Then, set aside time to study a little bit every day.

- **Read all the questions carefully.** Be sure you know what is being asked.

- **Skip any questions** you don't know how to answer right away. Mark them and come back later if you have time.

Glossary

atoms tiny building blocks that make up everything

crystals the shapes in which minerals form

explosives things that are used to blow things up

minerals solid substances found in nature

mining digging up materials from the ground

naturally happening in nature without help from people

ores rocks that have useful minerals inside them

rare not often found or seen

recycling turning something used or old into something new

substances certain kinds of material

Read More

Daly, Ruth. *How We Use Rocks and Minerals (Introduction to Earth's Resources).* New York: Crabtree Publishing Company, 2021.

Pettiford, Rebecca. *Minerals (Geology Genius).* Minneapolis: Jump! 2019.

Wood, Alix. *Get Hands-On with Rocks and Minerals (Hands-On Geology).* New York: Rosen Publishing, 2022.

Learn More Online

1. Go to **www.factsurfer.com** or scan the QR code below.
2. Enter "**Geology Minerals**" into the search box.
3. Click on the cover of this book to see a list of websites.

Index

aluminum 14
atoms 8–9, 28
crystals 8–9, 16
diamonds 24–25, 28
factories 12, 14, 18
food 16, 18
galena 9
gold 4, 22
gypsum 16

iron 18
metal 8, 14–15, 18, 22, 24
mining 12–13, 16, 20, 22
ores 12–14
quartz 8
recycling 26–27
rocks 4, 10, 12, 18, 20, 22, 24
salt 20–22, 28

About the Author

Ruth Owen has written hundreds of non-fiction books. She lives on the rocky Cornish coast in England and has always been fascinated by rocks.